HELLO CELLO POSITIONS!

3rd Position Book

for Young Cellists

By Jisoo Ok

First edition June 2020

ISBN 978-1-7350859-1-3

www.hellocellobooks.com

Publications by Jisoo Ok:

Hello Cello Positions! Second Position
Hello Cello Positions! Third Position
Hello Cello Positions! Fourth Position

Available at amazon.com

Accompaniment tracks available at hellocellobooks.com

Author's Note

While experienced cellists have developed a firm understanding of the importance of navigating the fingerboard through years of training, beginners, especially young students, often struggle with the process of learning and understanding fingerboard positions.

Despite years of searching for the right guide to teach the neck positions, I was unable to find a suitable book designed for young cellists that explained the positions in a comprehensive, yet fun and easy-to-understand, manner.

It is through my passion to help my cello students learn the positions in a simple and fun way that this book was born.

I would like to thank my amazing students, Emma, Alyssa, Juliet, Darcy and Aarika, for inspiring me to write this book! Thanks to Agnes Kwasniewska for introducing me to these wonderful students at the Virtuoso Suzuki Academy.

I am eternally grateful to all my former cello teachers - Kim Young-Suk, James Tennant, Natalia Pavlutskaya, Fred Sherry and Bonnie Hampton. I am thankful to Pamela Devenport for teaching Suzuki philosophies and methods of cello teaching with a unique and masterful approach.

Special thanks to my cousin, Isabel Kwon, a Juilliard trained cellist, for her advice and insights and to my brother-in-law John Ahn for helping me with editing and proofreading. Finally, to my family, my husband Hector, my son Santiago, my sister Krystal, and my parents for their love and support.

I had so much fun composing and arranging the pieces in this book!
I hope you have as much fun learning and playing them!

Enjoy!
Jisoo Ok

Content

Cello Map

Closed Hand Position
Half steps between each fingers

C G D A

C#	G#	Eb	Bb	1/2 postion
D	A	E	B	1st position
Eb	Bb	F	C	Lower 2nd position
E	B	F#	C#	Upper 2nd position
F	C	G	D	3rd position (Lower 3rd position)
F#	C#	G#	Eb	Upper 3rd position
G	D	A	E	4th position
Ab	Eb	Bb	F	Upper 4th position
A	E	B	F#	
Bb	F	C	G	
B	F#	C#	G#	

Common Enharmonic Notes
(Different names for the same note)
C# = Db
D# = Eb
F# = Gb
G# = Ab
A# = Bb

Third Positions

Lower 3rd Position

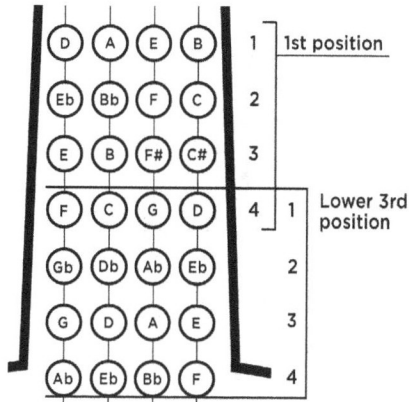

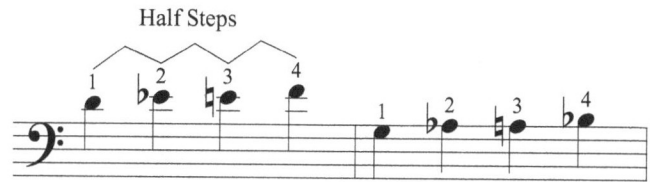

Extended 3rd Position

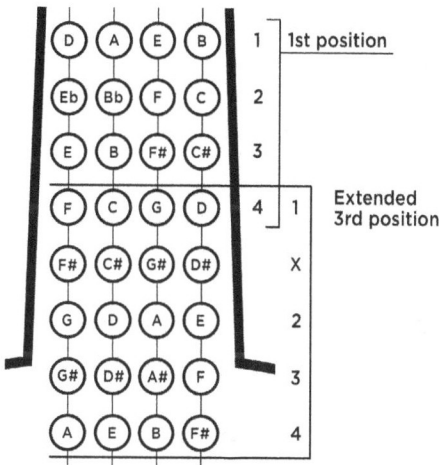

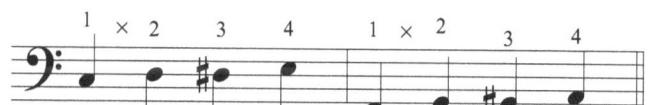

Upper 3rd Position

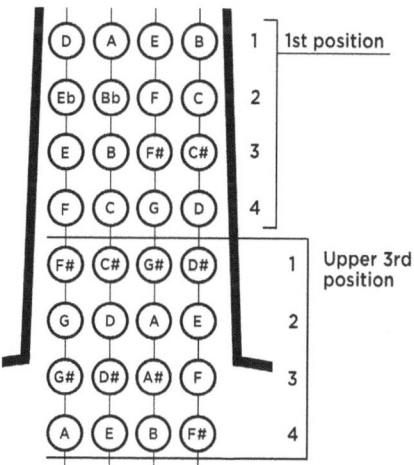

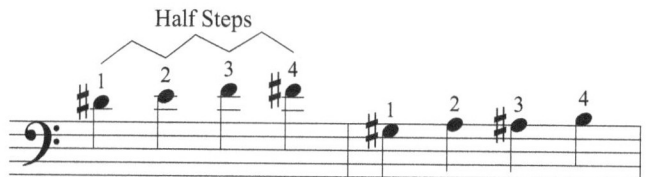

Hello Lower 3rd Position on A string!

Lower 3rd Position

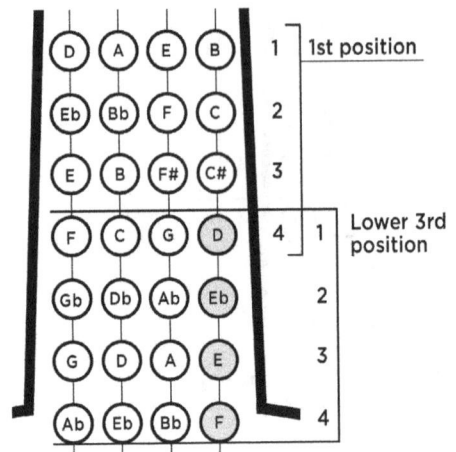

D   D   D   D   E♭   E   F

Hi There!

Musical Spelling Bee

Let's name the notes!

Sunrise

Sleepy Sloth

Always check the
key signature

Lazy Cat

Puppy Nap

Sneaky Kitty

Backyard Adventure

Sunset

Hello Lower 3rd Position on D string!

Lower 3rd Position

G G G G Ab A Bb

1st position

2

3

Lower 3rd position

Hi There!

Musical Spelling Bee

Let's name the notes!

Sunrise

Silly Goose

Puppy Nap

Following You

Dancing Panda Bear

London Bridge

English Folk Song

Hush Little Baby

Traditional American

Hello Lower 3rd Position on G string!

Hi There!

Musical Spelling Bee

Let's name the notes!

Sunrise

Sleepy Sloth

Sneaky Kitty

Hello Lower 3rd Position on C string!

Lower 3rd Position

| 0 | 3 | 1 | | 1 | 2 | 3 | 4 |

G　G　F　　F　G♭　G　A♭

Hi There!

Musical Spelling Bee

Let's name the notes!

Sunrise

Lazy Cat

Big Water Buffalo

Owl and the Night Sky

My First Camping Trip

Harmonics, Ones and Fours

Saraband

from Suite in D minor

George Handel
(1685–1759)

Lento

Hello Extended 3rd Position on A string!

Extended 3rd Position

D   D   D   D   E   F   F#

Hot Cross Buns

Traditional

Mary Had a Little Lamb

Traditional

Let's name the notes!

Climbing up to the Tree House

Silly Goose

On and Off

Hello Extended 3rd Position on D string!

Extended 3rd Position

G G G G A A# B

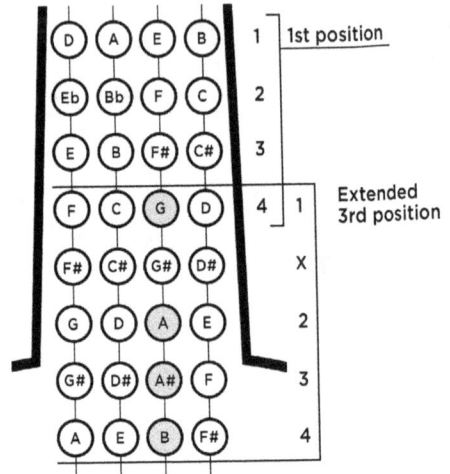

Hot Cross Buns

Traditional

Mary Had a Little Lamb

Traditional

Let's name the notes!

Climbing up to the Tree House

Cousin Jacques

Snack Time

Hello Extended 3rd Position on G string!

Extended 3rd Position

0 4 1 1 × 2 3 4

C C C C D D# E

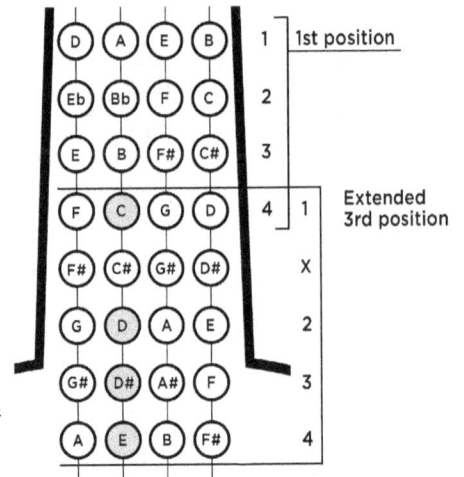

Hot Cross Buns

Traditional

4 2 × 1

Mary Had a Little Lamb

Traditional

4 2 × 1

Let's name the notes!

4 2 × 1

Climbing up to the Tree House

0 1 1 × 2 4 3

Very Sleepy Sloth

Feeling Lucky

Hello Extended 3rd Position on C string!

Extended 3rd Position

| 0 | 2 × 1 | 1 × 2 | 3 | 4 |

G G F F G G# A

Hot Cross Buns

Traditional

4 2 × 1

Mary Had a Little Lamb

Traditional

4 2 × 1

Let's name the notes!

4 2 × 1

Climbing up to the Tree House

0 1 1 × 2 4 3

Frère Jacques

French Folk Song

The Wheels on the Bus

Traditional

26

Hello Upper 3rd Position on A string!

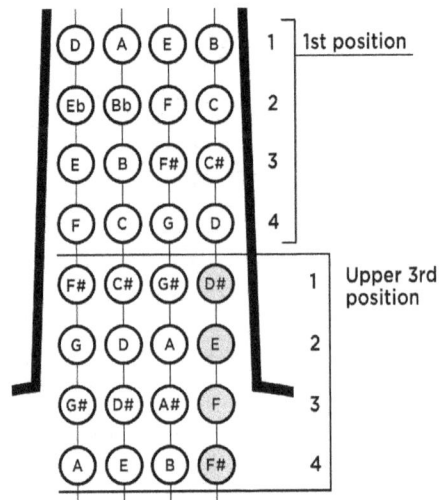

Lower 3rd Pos.

Upper 3rd Position

D   D   D#   D#   E   F   F#

Name Tag

Let's name the notes!

Mini Exploration

D sharp vs. D natural

Sleepy Sloth

Spring Time

Hello Upper 3rd Position on D string!

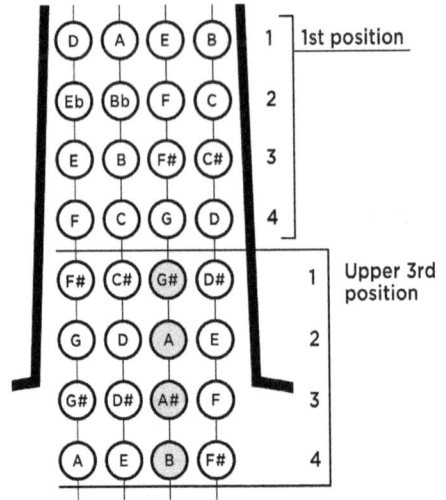

Name Tag

Let's name the notes!

Mini Exploration

G sharp vs. G natural

Little Goose

Pink Lemonade

Hello Upper 3rd Position on G string!

Upper 3rd Position

0   2   1   2   3   4

D   D   C#   D   D#   E

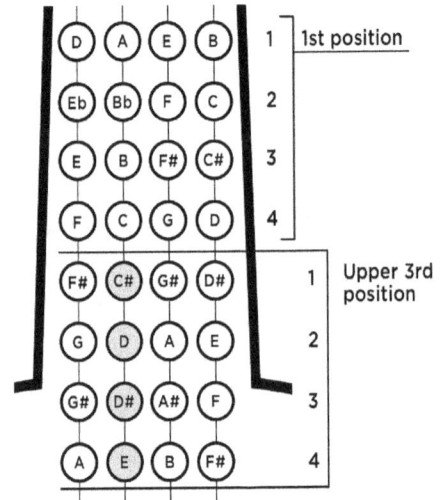

Name Tag

2   4   1

Let's name the notes!

Mini Exploration

4   2   1   3   1   3

C sharp vs. C natural

4   2   1   4   2 × 1

Lazy Cat

Thousands of Lilies

Hello Upper 3rd Position on C string!

Upper 3rd Position

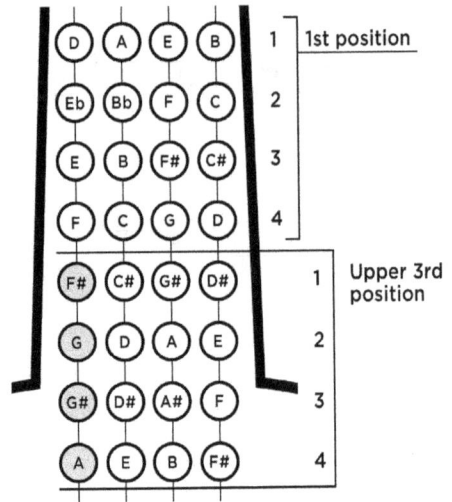

0	2	1	2	3	4

G   G   F#   G   G#   A

Name Tag

Let's name the notes!

Mini Exploration

F sharp vs. F nautral

Mary Lost a Little Lamb

Dancing Panda Bear

3rd Position Review Party!

Por Una Cabeza

Carlos Gardel
(1890-1935)

Bingo

Traditional

Overture
from William Tell

Gioachino Rossini
(1792-1868)

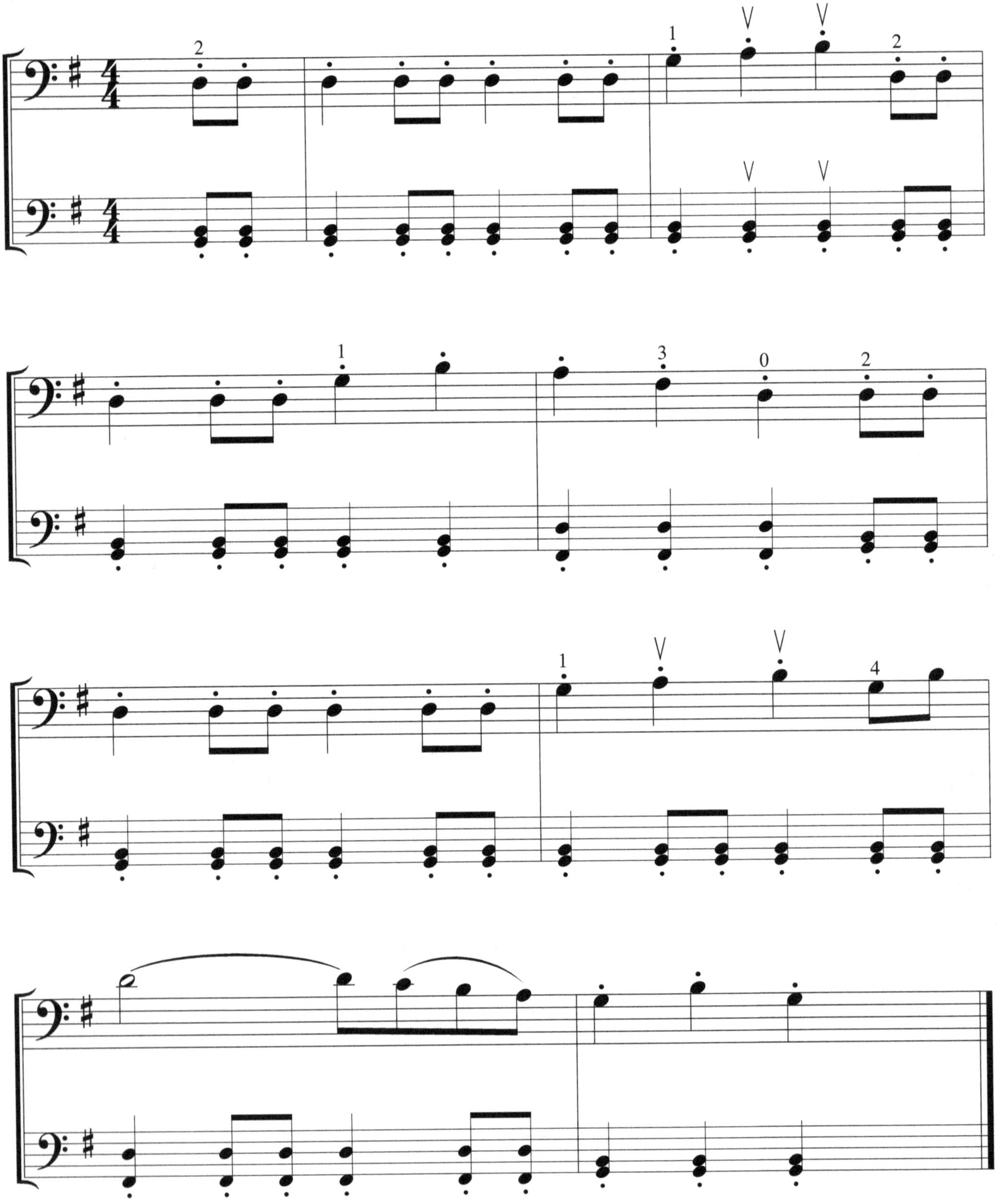

Ode to Joy
Ludwig van Beethoven
(1770-1827)

Lascia Ch'io Pianga
from Rinaldo
George Handel
(1685–1759)

Largo

2nd & 3rd Position Review Party!

Carnival of Venice

Neopolitan Song

Greensleeves

English Folk Song

Ein Mädchen oder Weibchen

from Magic Flute

Wolfgang Amadeus Mozart
(1756-1791)

He's a Jolly Good Fellow

Traditional

Watlz
from Sleeping Beauty

Pyotr Ilyich Tchaikovsky
(1840-1893)

Auld Lang Syne

Scottish Folk Song

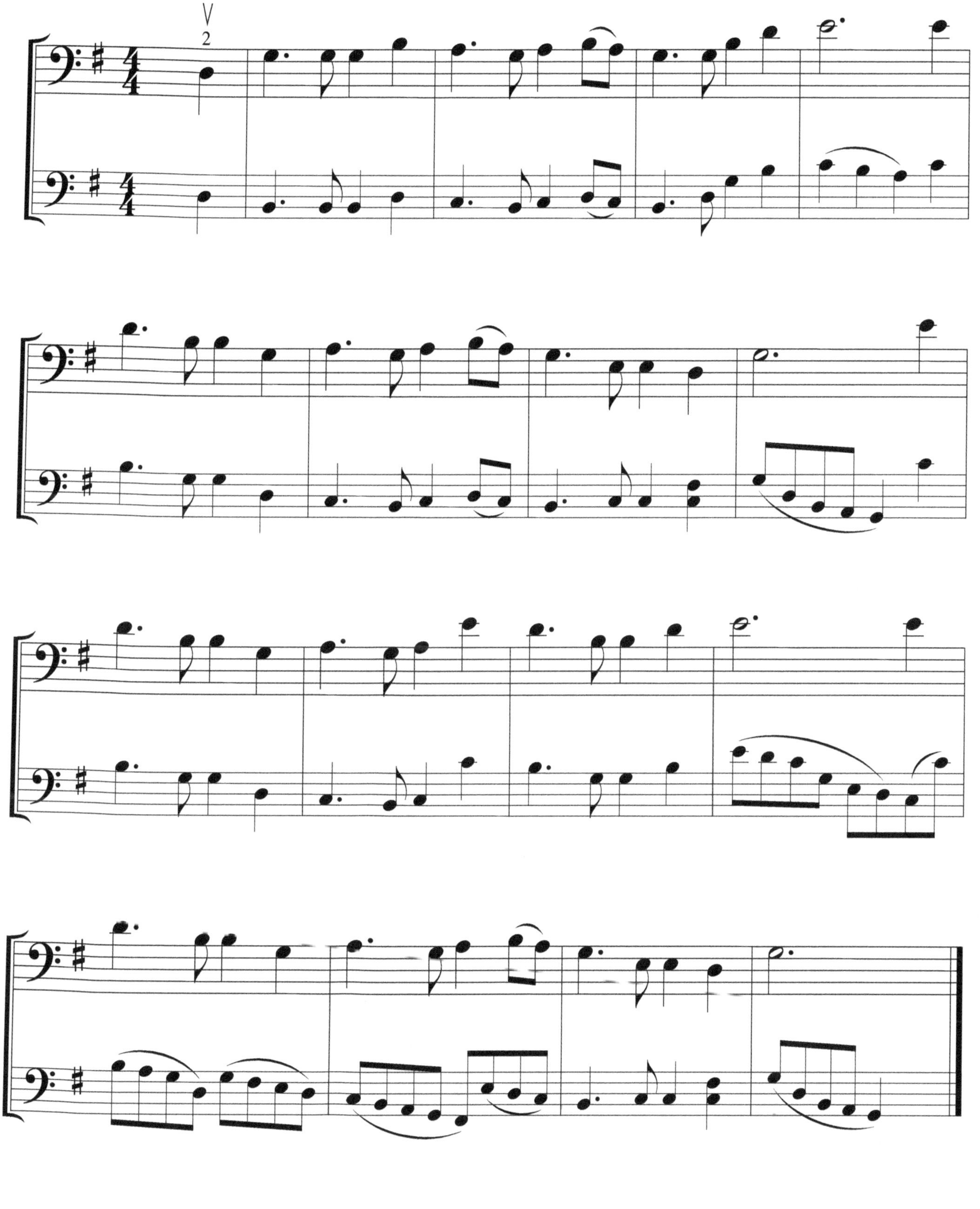

About the Author

As a Latin Grammy nominee, **Jisoo Ok** enjoys a multi-faceted and vibrant musical career as a cellist, festival director, arranger, orchestrator, recording artist and educator of classical and tango music.

Jisoo is deeply committed to exploring connections with musicians from other backgrounds and disciplines. This deep commitment can be seen in her collaborations with distinguished artists, such as latin jazz clarinetist Paquito D'Rivera, tango pianist Pablo Ziegler, bandoneonist Hector Del Curto, jazz violinist Regina Carter and bassist Ron Carter.

She has performed at prestigious venues and festivals, such as Carnegie Hall, Aspen Music Festival, La Jolla Music SummerFest, the Chautauqua Institute, Mondavi Center for the Performing Arts, Blue Note and National Concert Hall in Taiwan. As a soloist, she has performed with Rochester Philharmonic Orchestra and Lancaster Symphony Orchestra.

Her arrangements, orchestrations and transcriptions have been performed by top orchestras, such as Rochester Philharmonic Orchestra, St. Louis Symphony, Vermont Symphony Orchestra, Lancaster Symphony Orchestra, Billings Symphony Orchestra, Aspen Music Festival Chamber Orchestra and Stowe Tango Music Festival Orchestra.

Jisoo's dedication as a teacher can be seen in the success of her cello students, who have won numerous competitions and were accepted to Manhattan School of Music, New England Conservatory, Indiana University, The Juilliard School Pre-College, All-National Honors Orchestra and All-New York State Orchestra. She teaches privately and at the Virtuoso Suzuki Academy in Long Island, NY.

Jisoo was born in Seoul, Korea and raised in New Zealand. She has participated in master classes with Janos Starker, Bernard Greenhouse, Paul Katz, Laurence Lesser and Anner Bylsma. She received her Bachelor's and Master's degrees from The Juilliard School, studying with Bonnie Hampton and Fred Sherry. She studied chamber music with Itzhak Perlman and Robert Mann.

She is the co-founder and co- director of the Stowe Tango Music Festival, the premier tango music festival in the United States.

www.okcellist.com